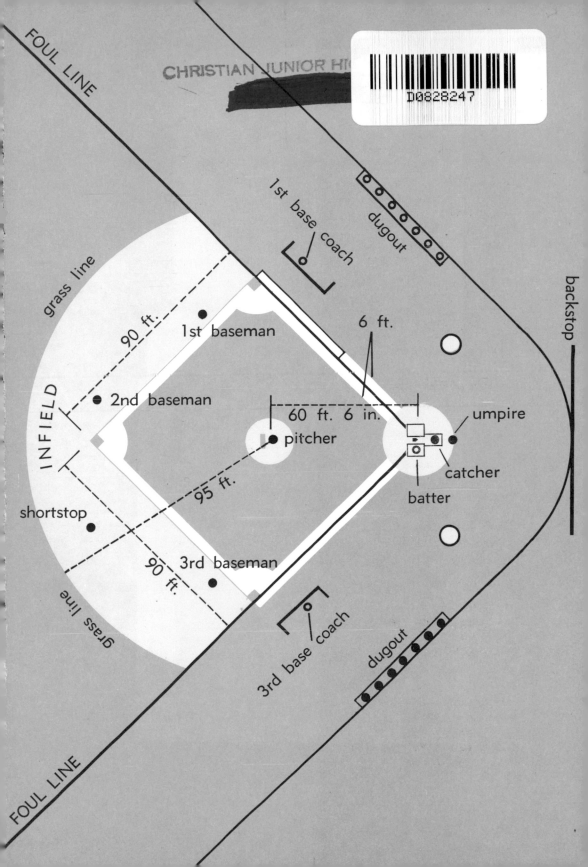

FOUL LINE

CHRISTIAN JUNIOR HIGH

1st base coach

dugout

grass line

90 ft.

1st baseman

6 ft.

INFIELD

2nd baseman

60 ft. 6 in.

pitcher

umpire

95 ft.

catcher

batter

shortstop

90 ft.

3rd baseman

backstop

3rd base coach

dugout

grass line

FOUL LINE

WILLIE MAYS
BASEBALL SUPERSTAR

★ ★ ★ ★ ★ ★ ★ ★ ★ ★ ★

BY SAM AND BERYL EPSTEIN

ILLUSTRATED BY VICTOR MAYS

GARRARD PUBLISHING COMPANY
CHAMPAIGN, ILLINOIS

Sports Consultant:
COLONEL RED REEDER
Former Member of the West Point Coaching Staff
and Special Assistant to the West Point
Director of Athletics

Acknowledgment:

Lines from the song "Amazin' Willie
Mays" on page 55 are reproduced by
permission of Samuel C. Florman.

Library of Congress Cataloging in Publication Data

Epstein, Samuel, 1909–
    Willie Mays: baseball superstar

    SUMMARY: A biography of the record-setting base-
ball player who is one of three in the game's history
to hit 600 home runs.
     1. Mays, Willie, 1931–   —Juvenile literature.
[1. Mays, Willie, 1931–   2. Baseball–Biography]
I. Epstein, Beryl Williams, 1910–   joint author.
II. Mays, Victor, 1927–   ill.   III. Title.
GV865.M38E67   796.357′092′4 [B] [92] 74–20954
ISBN 0–8116–6671–9

796.357
EPS

Photo credits:

United Press International: pp. 3, 31, 38 (bottom), 48,
    53, 66, 76, 79, 84 (both), 88, 91 (both), 94
Wide World: pp. 18, 38 (top), 62 (all), 71

Contents

1. Born to Play Baseball

"He was born to play baseball!"

That's what people said about Willie Mays from the very first.

"His daddy's a fine outfielder," they said. "His granddaddy was a fine pitcher. His mother was a high-school track star. So when little Willie grows up, he's bound to be out there throwing and catching and racing around those bases!"

Willie Mays was born May 6, 1931, in a suburb of Birmingham, Alabama. His father worked in a steel mill and played on the mill's all-black baseball team.

Some people thought *Willie* was a nickname for William, his father's name. But it wasn't. It was the name his young parents had given him.

He was about a year old when his father bought him his first ball. Then, every night, his father rolled the ball across the floor to his baby son.

"Now you pitch it back!" he said.

At first Willie only pushed at the ball. But soon he was picking it up and throwing it. He loved the game. Sometimes he cried when his father said, "Time to stop for supper."

When Willie was old enough to walk, his father and grandfather began taking him to ball games. Willie sat in the stands with his grandfather one day when his father's team was playing.

"You want to know why folks call your father Kitty-Kat?" Willie's grandfather asked him. "Then you watch him catch."

Willie knew what a catch was. Baseball terms were among the first words he had learned.

"See how he pounced on that ball?" his grandfather said a minute later. "Quick and graceful as a cat, wasn't he?"

"Great catch!" people shouted. "Yay, Kitty-Kat!"

"Yay, Kitty-Kat!" Willie yelled in his high squeaky voice.

The fans around him laughed. There was something about Willie Mays, even then, that made people feel good, that made them want to laugh.

Willie was still very young when his parents were divorced. Then he went to live with his Aunt Sarah and her husband in the Birmingham suburb of Fairfield. Their neat white house was a happy home for him. His father lived nearby and ate his meals there.

One day Willie's father took him along

when his steel mill team played out of town. After the game the fans collected some money for the players, and the players divided it among themselves. Each man got a few dollars.

Willie had never known men could earn money for playing baseball. "That seemed to me just about the nicest idea anyone ever thought up!" he said long afterward.

At school he found other boys who liked to play ball. One of them, Charley Willis, became his best friend. When they played together, one of them pitched and did all the fielding. The other batted. Then they changed sides.

By the time Willie was ten, he was playing on sandlot teams with boys five years older than he was.

Willie's hero was the Yankee center fielder Joe DiMaggio. He tried to stand and swing and hit just the way DiMaggio did.

"Call me DiMag!" he told Charley Willis. "I'm going to be just like him."

His father and grandfather hoped Willie might become a professional ballplayer on some black team. Professional teams were either all-white or all-black in those days.

So the two men tried to teach the boy all they knew. They were proud of how fast he learned.

"We'll play a pepper game," Kitty-Kat told Willie one afternoon. He had a bat in his hand. "Throw me the ball, and I'll bunt it back."

Willie threw. His father bunted. The ball landed six feet to Willie's right. He ran over and picked it up.

"Couldn't you get there before the ball landed?" Kitty-Kat asked. "Try again."

That time he bunted toward Willie's left. Willie watched the ball sail through the air. He got under it. He made a clean catch.

"That's better," Kitty-Kat said. "We're going to do a lot of this," he told Willie. "It's the best thing I know for developing speed. It trains a player's feet and hands and eyes too."

Willie was fourteen when his father said, "Our team will be short a man this afternoon. Want to fill in for us?"

Willie's eyes opened wide. "Would the other men let me?"

Some of the players weren't happy when Kitty-Kat's skinny son showed up with him. They changed their minds after a few minutes.

"That kid's all right!" one said.

When they divided up the money collected after the game, they gave him a share.

"I'm a professional!" Willie said. "I earned money for playing ball."

2. On His Way

From then on Willie often played with his father's team. Usually his share was ten or twelve dollars after a Saturday afternoon game.

He felt rich. Now he could pay for two of the things he liked best, ice cream sodas and Western movies.

He could also buy a lot of presents. Some were for what he called his "other family." This was his mother and her second husband and their children. Willie was very fond of his young half brothers and half sisters.

His high school had no baseball team—only football and basketball teams. Willie made both in his freshman year. He was thinner and lighter than most football players. But he could run and pass.

"He's the greatest forward passer I've ever seen," the school coach told Willie's father.

One day Willie's friend, Charley Willis, was badly hurt in a game.

"I guess I don't like football so much after all," Willie said.

He still liked basketball however. His timing and precision helped his team win the county championship. In his sophomore year he was the county's top scorer.

Each season Willie also pitched for neighborhood and semipro baseball teams.

One hot day he clouted the winning home run after nine hard innings. As he crossed the plate, he fell to the ground, unconscious.

His father was bending over him when he opened his eyes.

"You were bearing down too hard out there," Kitty-Kat said. "From now on you'll play in the outfield. It's easier on you. Besides," he added, grinning, "fielders get to play every day."

Willie was convinced. He gave up pitching.

A very important thing happened in the all-white world of major-league baseball the year Willie was fifteen. The Brooklyn Dodgers hired a black player for their Montreal Royals farm team. He was Jackie Robinson, who had starred in the Negro National League.

Many white players and fans insulted Jackie at first. But he became the star of the Royals. He moved up to the Dodgers the next year and helped them win the pennant. He was named Rookie of the Year.

14

Suddenly big-league managers were busy scouting black teams. The all-white rule of the majors had been broken. Now young black players knew that if they made good on a black professional team, they might catch the eye of a major-league scout.

Kitty-Kat knew it too. He went to see an old friend, Piper Davis. Davis managed the Birmingham Barons of the Negro National League.

"Piper Davis says he'll take a look at you," Kitty-Kat told Willie afterward.

Willie was scared. He was also excited.

Davis watched him throw for a while. Then he sent a Baron out to pitch to him.

"Don't try to copy DiMaggio!" Davis yelled a moment later, as Willie swung. "You're not big enough." He shook his head. "He's got a lot to learn," he told Kitty-Kat.

"You could teach him," Kitty-Kat said.

"Yes, I could." Davis called Willie over.

"Do you want to play with the Barons? I can pay only $70 a month. Is that enough?"

Willie looked at his father and nodded. Kitty-Kat nodded back.

"It's enough," Willie said.

No contract was signed. But at the end of his sophomore year in high school, Willie's professional playing career really began.

He could no longer play with his amateur school teams, but he still attended most of his classes. And he studied hard to make up the work he missed when the Barons were on the road.

Davis used Willie in every position. He also did his best to correct Willie's mistakes and cure his weaknesses.

"Don't throw him anything but curves," Davis told his pitchers during practice. "He can't hit them, and he's got to learn."

One day the Barons' center fielder was hurt.

16

"You take his place, Willie," Davis said.

Pepper games with Kitty-Kat had trained Willie for that position. Davis watched him make catches most players would have missed.

"You're our center fielder from now on," Davis decided.

Willie enjoyed riding around on the Barons' bus with the other players. He didn't even mind when they had to sleep on the bus. The older men teased him and played jokes on him. He made them laugh because he was always laughing.

When he returned home, he told everybody about his adventures.

"I saw a major-league game," he said. "We had an afternoon off, and I watched the St. Louis Browns play the Boston Red Sox. You should have seen that Boston hitter, Ted Williams! I never knew a man could swing a bat so hard and so fast."

Willie also went on a barnstorming tour

with a pickup team of some of the country's best black players. Roy Campanella had organized it. He was one of the black players already hired by the major leagues.

"Campy is a great guy!" Willie told his friends. "And Monte Irvin—he's the best! And I went one for two against Satch Paige!"

Satchel Paige had long been the greatest pitcher in the black leagues.

"Some men have tried for years to get a hit off Satch," Davis said proudly. "Willie did it the first time."

But Willie was disappointed when the second season with the Barons was over.

"The major-league scouts who came to some of our games never even talked to me," he told Kitty-Kat. "I guess I'm just not good enough."

"They know you have to finish high school," Kitty-Kat said. "Besides, Campanella and the others they've signed were Negro

Satchel Paige winds up for a pitch. Sixteen-year-old Willie got a hit the first time he faced the famous black pitcher.

National stars a long time before they made it."

"Sure," Willie said. "And that means a lot of their best years are already behind them. Me, I'd like to hit the majors while my best years are still ahead of me."

One day early the next season, a stranger spoke to him in the dressing room.

"From the stands you looked skinny,"

the stranger said. "But now I can see you've got a lot of muscle on you."

"I guess I have," Willie said. He grinned.

The stranger couldn't help grinning back. "I'll be watching you play Tuscaloosa tomorrow," he said before he left.

The stranger was Eddie Montague, a Giant scout. The New York Giants had sent him to Birmingham to look at the Barons' first baseman, Alonzo Perry.

Montague telephoned the Giants' office after he left Willie.

"I don't think Perry will do for us," he said. "But the Barons have a nineteen-year-old center fielder who is the greatest ballplayer I've ever seen! He's got a great arm. He's got speed. And he's a fantastic fielder. His name is Willie Mays."

"Never heard of him," the Giant official said. "But if he's that good, you'd better sign him up."

Montague found Willie as soon as Willie walked on the field at Tuscaloosa.

"Would you like to play professional ball?" he asked.

Willie could have answered that he had been playing good professional ball for some time. But his Aunt Sarah had taught him to be polite. Besides, he didn't want to spoil the chance he'd been waiting for.

"Yes, sir," he said. "I'd like to."

"Good," the man said. "I'm Eddie Montague of the Giant organization. I'll talk to the Barons' owner about buying your contract."

"What contract?" Willie asked. "The Barons don't own me."

"Then where will you be tomorrow?" Montague asked.

Willie told him. Montague called him the next day.

"You'll have to talk to my Aunt Sarah," Willie said. "I'll put her on."

Montague was surprised to be dealing with a ballplayer's aunt. "How big a bonus does Willie want to sign a contract?" he asked.

"Five thousand dollars," Aunt Sarah said briskly.

"I'll check with my office and be at your place this afternoon," Montague told her.

It was a great occasion. Kitty-Kat hurried home from the mill to be there. One of Willie's half sisters came too. Willie wanted both his families to share this day.

Montague spread the contract out on the dining room table. Everybody read it. Then Willie signed his name while the others watched. Kitty-Kat had to sign too, because Willie was a minor.

Afterward Montague gave Willie his bonus check for $5,000. Willie learned later that the Giants had also given the Barons $10,000. "The Giants are a great organization," he always said.

"You can go on playing with the Barons until your graduation," Montague said. "Then you'll join our farm team in Trenton, New Jersey."

Willie stared at his check after Montague left.

"This will buy a lot of ice cream sodas!" he said.

Everybody laughed. Aunt Sarah hugged him. She knew Willie would spend most of his money on his two families.

"Of course the Trentons aren't much," Kitty-Kat said, grinning. "Only a Class B team."

"That's right," Willie said. "And the Barons play Triple A ball and everybody knows it. Trenton will be a real come-down."

Then he laughed. "But I'm on my way to the Giants!"

"Yes, son," Kitty-Kat said. "You're on your way."

3. The Say-Hey Kid

The train trip north to Trenton was long and lonely. Willie had plenty of time to ask himself questions.

Would the other players call him names and insult him because he was black? he wondered. Would the Trenton manager use him only as a substitute?

The questions were answered as soon as he arrived. The other members of the team were friendly.

"Hear you're pretty good," one said.

"Glad you got here, Mays," the general manager, Bill McKechnie, Jr., said. "You'll be our center fielder."

Then Willie struck out his first 22 times at bat. Suddenly he was afraid he wasn't a good ballplayer after all.

"Why can't I hit this pitching?" he asked McKechnie.

"Don't worry about your hitting," McKechnie said. "You're our center fielder. Just go up there and take your swings."

Willie felt better. The next time he walked up to the plate he swung—and hit! He kept on hitting. His average soared to .380.

Now, once again, Willie went around grinning. His teammates grinned back. And they always laughed at one thing he did.

"Say, hey!" Willie said when he couldn't remember someone's name.

"That's our Say-Hey Kid!" his teammates said.

The fans began to call Willie that too. And they liked to watch him leap for a high catch or race down the base lines.

One day in the team's bus, McKechnie sat down beside Willie.

"Suppose you've just pitched one-and-two to a hitter whose weakness is high inside," McKechnie said. "Where would you pitch him next?"

"I'm not a pitcher," Willie said. "Why do you ask me a question like that?"

"Because the only way to be a smart hitter is to try to think like a pitcher," McKechnie said.

That was a new idea to Willie. He had always tried to learn how to hit harder, run faster, and field better. But baseball had always been just a game he loved to play. Now McKechnie seemed to be telling him it was a science and an art. He was saying Willie should think about it.

"Think, Willie," McKechnie said. "I want an answer."

From then on McKechnie often sat beside Willie and asked him questions.

"The more I learn, the more I find out I don't know," Willie thought. But he began to play ball with his brains as well as his body.

He watched to see what his own pitcher was going to throw. He knew the kind of pitch often determined the direction a hit ball would take. This helped him make difficult catches.

He also tested the outfield turf every day. He knew its condition determined whether a ball would bounce or just roll a few feet and stop. His test helped him decide whether he should play back for a lively grounder or play in close to grab the dead balls.

Willie ended that 1950 season with an average of .353 for the 81 games he had played. His small total of four home runs showed that he wasn't hitting very hard most of the time. But he was so fast on the base paths that he scored twenty doubles and eight triples. And he stole seven bases.

His cap often flew off his head as he ran.

"Willie ran out from under his cap again!" some fan always shouted.

The next spring he was told to report to the Triple A Minneapolis Millers, the Giants' top farm team.

The Millers trained in Sanford, Florida. So did the Giants. Soon the Millers had a visit from Horace Stoneham, the Giants' owner, and Leo Durocher, their new manager.

Durocher looked at Willie. "We got quite a report on you from Trenton," he said.

"What did it say?" Willie asked.

"It said your cap keeps flying off," Durocher said and walked away laughing.

When the Millers went to Minneapolis to start their season, Willie felt far away

Willie Mays in the uniform of the Millers. The young rookie received a hearty welcome from Minneapolis fans.

from his Southern home. But the Millers welcomed him warmly. They cheered his spectacular catches and his base running. He began to hit better than ever. Soon his average rose past .400!

During one game he sent a line drive right through the wooden fence at the end of the field.

"We'll paint a white circle around that hole," one fan said. "And we'll keep it forever in honor of Willie Mays."

On May 25, in that year 1951, Willie had an afternoon off. He headed for a Western double-feature. When the lights went on between movies, a man came on stage.

"If Willie Mays is here," the man said, "his manager wants him at the hotel."

Willie jumped up and ran. Had something happened to his father? he wondered. Or to his Aunt Sarah?

The Millers' manager smiled when Willie dashed into his room. "Congratulations!" he said. "You're going to the big leagues!"

Willie thought he was joking. "Who says so?" he asked.

"Leo Durocher," the manager said. "I just talked to him on the phone. He wants you in New York right away."

Willie thought, "I'm not ready!" He felt he still hadn't learned enough about the science of baseball. He couldn't forget his bad slump in his first days at Trenton. He didn't want to risk another one, in the big leagues this time.

"Tell Durocher I'm not coming," he said.

The manager stared at him. "What's the matter with you?" he said.

"I can't hit that big-league pitching," Willie muttered.

"All right," the manager said finally. "If you're serious I'll call him."

He got Durocher on the line. "Willie doesn't want to come," he said. "He'll tell you himself." He handed the telephone to Willie.

Durocher was shouting angrily even before Willie said hello. Willie waited until Durocher stopped for breath. Then he said, "But I can't play that kind of ball. I can't hit."

"What are you hitting now?" Durocher shouted.

Willie told him. "Four seventy-seven," he said.

There was a long silence. Durocher didn't say he had already heard about that .477 average. He also didn't tell Willie that the Giant center fielder was hitting a poor .229.

"Do you think you could hit .250 for me?" Durocher asked quietly.

Willie thought about it. He supposed he could hit that well even in the big leagues. "I guess so," he said.

"Then come to New York!" Durocher shouted, and he hung up.

4. Number 24

Willie had no time to pack. He just managed to get on a plane to New York that afternoon. A taxi took him to the Giants' headquarters.

Horace Stoneham, the Giants' owner, came out from behind his desk to shake Willie's hand.

"Glad you could make it, Mays," he said. "We know Minneapolis doesn't want to lose you," he went on. "So we're putting a special notice in the papers there. It apologizes to your fans for taking you away from them."

Willie had never heard of a ball club doing that before.

"But what if I don't make it, Mr. Stoneham?" he burst out.

Stoneham answered him calmly. "Don't worry," he said. "Our scouts have done a lot of checking on you. We know what you can do."

"Well," Willie said, "I just hope you won't be sorry. I hope I can get in a few games, and maybe help the team."

"A few games!" Stoneham repeated. "Didn't they tell you? You're starting at center field for us tonight in Philadelphia."

The next few hours flashed by like lightning.

Stoneham told Doc Bowman, the Giants' trainer, to take Willie to Philadelphia and to get him the clothes he needed.

On the train Bowman talked about the Giants' chances.

"We were all hoping for the pennant

this year," he said. "Then we had that bad start, with eleven losses in a row. We've done better lately, but we're still way down in fifth place."

At the Philly clubhouse Willie was handed a Giant uniform. It had orange piping and black lettering. The number on the back was 24. Photographers took his picture. Suddenly it was game time. Willie trotted out onto the field with the team.

His hands were damp when he came up to bat. Three times he swung wildly.

"Out!" the umpire signaled.

Willie struck out his other four times at bat too.

In the field he ran for a ball that right fielder Monte Irvin was about to catch. Willie crashed into him. The ball got away. The Philly batter had a double.

But the Giants won 8–5 that night. One sportswriter said they had been "inspired by their flashy rookie star, Willie Mays."

A few words of advice from Manager Leo Durocher (above) before Willie's first game for the Giants. Below, Willie slides home in a game with the Cubs.

In the next two games Willie also went hitless. Both times the Giants won.

When the team returned to New York, Willie faced the Giants' home fans for the first time. His record was 0 for 12.

He couldn't understand why the fans cheered when his name was announced in the batting order.

The Giants were playing the Boston Braves that night. The Braves' pitcher was the great Warren Spahn.

Spahn's first pitch to Willie was a fast ball. Willie swung. His bat connected! The ball flew toward the stands. Willie tore around the bases. His first major-league hit was a home run!

Willie hoped his slump had ended. It hadn't. The day his record sank to 1 for 26, he sat down beside his locker and cried.

Leo Durocher found him there. "What are you crying about?" he growled.

"I told you I couldn't hit this pitching!" Willie said. "Please send me back down."

"So you didn't get a hit today," Durocher said. "So what? Have we been winning games since you came up? Sure we have. So you'll go on being our center fielder, and that's that.

"But pull up your pants," Durocher ordered. "They're hanging down almost to your ankles. That makes the umpires think your strike zone goes down that far. Pull them up and you'll get two hits tomorrow!"

The next day Willie pulled up his pants. He got a single and a triple off the Pirates. Then, against the Cardinals, he got two doubles and scored the victorious Giants' only run.

His slump was finally over. He was off on a hitting streak. And many of his hits were home runs. Once he had six homers in a row. He was also covering center field "like a tent," as one sportswriter put it.

"He's the best rookie I've ever seen," Durocher bragged.

Willie's spirits rose with his success.

"I guess I kind of bubbled," he wrote long afterward. "The older guys treated me like a happy kid—which is what I was."

On the road Willie roomed with Monte Irvin. He had always admired the big right fielder. Now Irvin was like a wise older brother to him.

"Let's get a soda," Willie would often say in their room.

"You've already had enough sodas today," Irvin would reply.

Willie grinned when he could answer, "But I got more hits than you today. So I'm Boss of the Room. Come on!"

Willie loved the Boss-of-the-Room game he played with Irvin. The loser had to buy as many sodas as the winner could drink that day.

In New York, Willie lived with a warm-hearted landlady who treated him like a son. She made sure he got to bed early. She fed him plenty of steak and potatoes and milk. At dinner time she usually had to call him in from the street. Willie spent most of his spare time there, playing stickball with small boys.

"What's a Giant doing, playing with kids and a broomstick and a little rubber ball?" a news photographer asked him once.

"Say, hey!" Willie said. "This is good training for my eyes." Then he grinned. "Besides," he said, "I just like to play ball."

By August the Giants were in second place, with only the Brooklyn Dodgers ahead of them. But most people thought that the Dodgers had the pennant sewed up. They had a lead of thirteen games.

Then the Dodgers began losing and the Giants kept on winning. The Giants had caught Willie's high spirits. On the afternoon of August 15, they faced the Dodgers on the field.

They had already lost twelve games to the Dodgers. This one was tied 1–1 in the eighth inning.

The Dodgers' powerful Carl Furillo came up to bat with only one out. There were men on first and third. Willie knew the right-handed Furillo usually hit to left field, so he moved in that direction.

But Furillo hit a fly into the wide gap Willie had left. Willie turned and ran at full speed, his gloved left hand high.

He was under the ball when it came down. As he shifted the ball to his right hand, he pivoted on his left foot. His spin brought him around in a half-circle, to face the infield.

The Giants' second baseman had moved into line for the catch. When he saw the ball coming at him like a bullet, he stepped aside and let it streak past him to land in the catcher's mitt. The catcher tagged the man sliding in from third.

For a long moment the stands were silent. Then the fans realized what had happened. They screamed. They shouted.

With that tremendous play Willie had put two men out and ended the inning.

"The greatest play I've ever seen," one Giant official said.

The Dodger manager shook his head. "I saw it and I still don't believe it," he said.

Time magazine called it "The Throw." In headlines all over the country, the Say-Hey Kid became "The Amazin' Mays." New York fans gave him a Willie Mays Day.

"I knew what this boy could do!" Durocher told everyone.

Willie still made mistakes. Once he belted

out a long one—and then failed to touch third base as he raced toward home. But most of the time he was playing great ball.

By mid-September the Giants were only six and a half games behind the Dodgers. At the season's end the two teams were tied for first place and had to go into a three-game play-off. Thousands of fans jammed the stands each day.

The Giants won the first game. The Dodgers took the second.

In the third game the Dodgers got a run in the first inning. The score was still Dodgers 1, Giants 0 in the sixth.

In the seventh inning the Giants made it a tie. Then the Dodgers got three runs for a 4–1 lead.

In the ninth inning the Giant player Alvin Dark singled. He moved to second on a hit by Don Mueller. He got home on a double by Whitey Lockman. But Mueller slid into third so hard that he sprained his ankle. Clint Hartung was sent in to run for him.

Now Hartung and Lockman were on base, and the score was Dodgers 4, Giants 2. Bobby Thomson walked up to the plate. Behind him, in the on-deck circle, Willie Mays was waiting.

"If the Dodgers walk Bobby, I'll be up," he thought.

Then the game and the pennant would depend on him!

Thomson took one strike. The Dodger pitcher hurled again. Willie's heart leaped into his throat as Thomson's bat cracked against leather.

The ball headed for the stands. Thomson and Lockman and Hartung all scored. The game was over. The pennant was won.

The happiest Giant in the clubhouse that day was Willie Mays. Somebody handed him a glass.

"No, thanks," Willie said. "I don't drink."

"But everybody's having champagne to celebrate!" the man said.

Willie took one swallow. One minute later he was sick.

"You'll feel better soon," a grinning teammate told him. "Then you can celebrate in your own way, with a couple of ice cream sodas."

After the excitement of that pennant-winning play-off, even the World Series with the Yankees was a letdown.

A strong hit, and Willie Mays is on his way to first base in the 1951 World Series.

The Giants took the first game 5–1. They lost the second and took the third 6–2. Willie had batted in one of those runs. But the Yankees took the other three games and won the championship.

The 1951 baseball season was over. Most fans said it had been one of the most exciting they had ever known.

It had certainly been a great season for Willie Mays and the Giants. And during the first Series game Willie had had a thrill he would never forget. For the first time he found himself on the same field with his hero, Joe DiMaggio.

"Come on, Willie," a photographer said. "We want a picture of you and DiMag together."

"You mean it?" Willie said.

Then he was actually standing beside the greatest center fielder of his day. He was actually talking to DiMaggio!

DiMaggio was 36 years old that day,

and about to retire. Willie Mays was 20 years old and just beginning his career.

But as Willie headed home that fall, it seemed that his career might end with his first season. The Korean War was going on. He knew he would soon be drafted into the army.

He wasn't going to let that spoil his homecoming, however. He had been named Rookie of the Year. He had earned $5,000 for the season and $5,000 World Series money. He planned to buy presents for everybody in both his families. And he was going to show Kitty-Kat how much his pepper game had improved.

5. Amazin' Willie Mays

Willie Mays exchanged his Giant uniform for an army uniform on May 29, 1952. Before that date he played in the first 34 games of the Giants' regular season. The Giants won 27 of them.

His last game before going into the army was against the Dodgers. Dodger fans as well as Giant fans rose and applauded when he came up to bat. Players of both teams were clapping too. It was their way of saying, "Good luck, Willie!"

After Willie left, one sportswriter said, "The Giant team is playing as if its heart were truly gone." In spite of its good start, the team finished in second place. The next year it dropped to fifth place.

In the army Willie served as an athletic instructor and played on his camp's ball team. He put on weight and muscle. He also learned something from one soldier he taught.

"That's no way to catch," Willie had told the man. The soldier had cupped his hands at his waist and let the ball drop into them.

Then Willie tried the "basket catch" himself and liked it. "I can get my throw off quicker," he said.

On March 2, 1954, Willie left the army. He flew straight to Phoenix, Arizona, where the Giants were training.

"Say, hey!" he shouted as he walked into the team's dressing room. "I'm here!"

The Giant pitcher, Sal Maglie, stared at him with a straight face. "Who's this?" he asked. "Some rookie?"

There were jokes and laughter in the Giant clubhouse once again. Headlines on sports pages all over the country said WILLIE'S BACK!

This would be Willie Mays's first full season with the team. "Is he really as good as he seemed in 1951?" people wondered.

Monte Irvin (left) welcomes the Giants' favorite rookie back from army service.

The Giants' opening game was with their great rival, the Dodgers. The score was tied 2–2 when Willie came to bat in the seventh inning.

Carl Erskine, the Dodger pitching ace, threw a fast ball that smoked its way to the plate. Willie drove it some 400 feet into the stands.

From then on he seldom let up. In an early game with Chicago, he broke a fourteenth inning tie with another game-winning homer. Late in May he got two home runs and batted in three more to give the Giants a 5–4 victory over Philadelphia.

In June the Giants passed the Dodgers and took first place. In early July they made a clean sweep of a three-game series against their Brooklyn foes. Willie had a homer in each of the first two games and two homers in the third. The final one was his 30th of the season.

Willie Mays had become a superstar. He was getting superstar treatment.

Sportswriters liked him and wrote hundreds of stories about him. They said he was decent, modest, and a "joyous boy." They called his ball playing "fantastic, incredible, the greatest."

Photographers wanted his picture almost every day too. One picture of him was on the cover of *Time* magazine.

And songwriters wrote songs about him. Part of the song called "Amazin' Willie Mays" went like this:

Who has that extra spark?
Who makes the game a lark?
Who brings me to the park?
Amazin' Willie Mays!

Sometimes Willie got tired of having to talk to so many sportswriters and pose for so many pictures. He was also asked to spend a lot of his spare time appearing on radio and television shows. But he knew the publicity about him helped sell tickets to the Giants' games. He was learning that big-league baseball was big business.

It was becoming big business for him too. Manufacturers offered him money for the right to use his picture in their ads.

Leo Durocher was worried. "Willie's too trusting and good-natured to know how to handle those businessmen," he said.

So Durocher asked two men to help Willie. One was Frank Forbes, an old-time athlete on the Giants' staff. The other was a business executive. Together they made sure Willie was paid fairly for the use of his name and for radio and television appearances.

Soon Willie was making more money than he'd ever dreamed of. Part of it helped support his two families. He enjoyed spending the rest. He bought expensive clothes, a fine record player, and hundreds of records. He bought a big car.

But Willie didn't keep all he bought. If someone admired one of his new monogrammed shirts, he said, "I want you to have it." Sometimes he took it off right there and gave it away.

He gave money away too, to his friends and even to people he scarcely knew.

By midseason, with Willie's help, the Giants had a comfortable lead in the pennant race.

Then a message reached Willie that his Aunt Sarah had died.

"I know you want to go home," Durocher said. "Forbes can go along to help out."

After the funeral Willie joined the team in Milwaukee. He still played as well as ever. "But," sportswriter Lee Greene wrote, "some of the spark had gone out of him, and suddenly the Giants stopped winning."

Their comfortable lead dropped to three

games. The Dodgers closed in on them. So did the Milwaukee Braves. Late in July Durocher took Willie aside.

"I want you to stop swinging for homers," he said.

Willie stared at him. "Why?" he asked.

"Look," Durocher said, "when you hit a ball out of the park it's a home run. But if you hit a long ball that doesn't go out of the park, it usually winds up in an outfielder's mitt. They know where you hit, and they lay for you."

"So what should I do?" Willie said.

"Stop swinging so hard," Durocher told him. "Then you can place the ball better. Move it around—to right—to center. That way you'll get on base more often. With your speed you'll score more often too. We need those extra base hits, Willie."

Willie could see it made sense.

"OK," he said. "I'll try."

He had hit 36 homers so far that year.

He hit only five more during the rest of the season. But his batting average climbed. And opposition runners often stayed glued to the bases, afraid of Willie's great throwing power. The Giants were winning again.

On August 8, the fans showered Willie with gifts on Willie Mays Day to show their appreciation and warm affection.

The pennant race was still tight. When the Giants lost three games to the Dodgers, their lead dropped to half a game.

But the next day Willie's bat exploded. He got four hits, and the Giants beat Philadelphia. That started a seven-game winning streak that put them three games ahead.

Then Willie got three hits against the Dodgers, for a 7–1 Giant win. And that clinched the pennant.

But when the season's last day arrived, the batting championship still wasn't settled. Willie was in the running with his teammate Don Mueller and the Dodgers' Duke Snider. Experts needed four figures to rate them:

Mueller .3426

Snider .3425

Mays .3422

The Giants played Philadelphia that day. The Phillies' pitcher, Robin Roberts, was one of the best.

Willie and Mueller both hit safely the first time up. Both were out on their second time at bat. Then Mueller flied out on his third trip to the plate, and Willie got a triple. Mueller flied out the next time too. Willie hit a two-bagger and put himself two hits ahead.

In the tenth inning Mueller got a double, while the cautious pitcher walked Willie. The fans screamed their anger over Willie's losing that chance to hit. But the game ended with Willie one hit ahead.

Then the news came that Duke Snider had gone hitless that day. Willie was the champion! The final standings were:

Mays   .345
Mueller .342
Snider   .341

New York fans gave the pennant-winning Giants a parade up Broadway. Willie grinned and waved from his car.

"Just seeing that man makes you feel good!" people said.

Even the fans, however, thought the Giants couldn't beat the powerful Cleveland Indians in the World Series.

The Giants thought they could. They did. They took the Indians in four straight games.

The thing most people talked about after that Series was a play Willie had made. It became famous as "The Catch."

"It's what I did with the ball after I

Mays came within one step of crashing into the bleacher wall in his famous catch of the 1954 World Series.

caught it that really counted," Willie himself said.

"The Catch" was made in the top of the eighth in the first Series game. The score was 2–2. Cleveland had men on first and second. The batter up was Vic Wertz, who had already singled twice and tripled once.

The Giant pitcher hurled the ball. Wertz connected squarely. The ball took off down center field in a high arc.

Willie was running at the crack of the bat. One look had told him where to go. As he reached the cinder track near the bleachers, he risked one more glance over his shoulder. The ball was right on course.

Still running, Willie held up his hands. The ball came down over his left shoulder, into his big mitt.

He pivoted to the left at the same time he shifted the ball. His right arm whipped back and then forward. The ball shot toward the cutoff man waiting at second base. It had so far to go that a Cleveland score seemed certain.

But the ball came so fast that the runner off first had to scramble back to that bag. And the runner from second had to stop at third.

The ball that had prevented a Cleveland run had traveled like a bullet over 300 feet!

Willie also scored four runs in the Series, drove in two more, and was walked four times.

At the season's end he was the league's slugging, as well as its batting champion. He was named its Most Valuable Player, and he had played in the All-Star game. He won awards as Athlete of the Year and Professional Athlete of the Year.

"He's not just as good as he seemed in 1951," people said now. "He's better! He's incredible! There's nobody like that amazin' Willie Mays!"

6. New York's Willie

Giant fans looked forward to the 1955 season.

"When Willie's on our team, we win," they said. "Remember 1951. Remember last year."

Except for a midseason slump, Willie showed them topflight ball at every game. Swinging for the fences again, he hit 51 home runs. No Giant had ever topped that total. In one stretch he homered seven times in six straight games.

Now Willie had also learned to place his long drives. Many that landed inside the

Mays jumps high off the ground to catch Williams's powerful drive to deep center.

park went for extra-base hits. He got thirteen triples that year to tie for the league lead. His runs-batted-in total climbed to 127. And he stole 24 bases.

In the All-Star game he got two singles out of three times at bat, scored two runs, and made three putouts. One putout robbed Ted Williams of a homer. The Boston slugger had hit a long drive to right center. Willie raced the ball to the fence, leaped high, and snared it a foot above the wire. His league won the game 6–5.

But the Giants wound up in third place that year. The Dodgers took the pennant.

"How did it happen?" Giant fans asked.

Horace Stoneham, the Giants' owner, thought he knew. He gave Willie a big raise. He fired Leo Durocher.

"Your new manager will be Bill Rigney," he told the team.

"When Leo left," Willie told a sportswriter, "it was like a kid losing his father. . . . I had to get used to Rigney."

Durocher had always taken Willie aside when he made mistakes. He had told him, in private, how the mistake could be corrected. Rigney was different.

During spring practice Willie once threw over the head of the cutoff man. He didn't often do that, and Rigney knew it. But Rigney yelled at him in front of the whole team.

"You gotta keep 'em down, Willie!" he shouted.

A sportswriter who heard him said, "Those two aren't going to get along. Willie won't do his best for Rigney."

"I played as hard for Rig as I played for any manager," Willie said later.

But while he was trying to get used to Rigney, he was also getting used to a whole new kind of life. In February 1956 he had married the beautiful Marghuerite Wendell.

The newlyweds moved into a big new apartment in an apartment house Willie had bought. Marghuerite's nine-year-old daughter from an earlier marriage lived with them. Willie had suddenly become a husband, a stepfather, and a landlord.

Willie had new responsibilities on the field too. He had outgrown his rookie days. As an older, more experienced player, he felt he should share his knowledge with younger men. A 1956 Giant rookie remembered, years later, how Willie had helped.

"Every day," Bill White recalled, "Willie would talk to me about the pitchers we were going to face: what they threw, what their ball did, what to expect in the clutch. He would tell me who you could steal on and who you couldn't, pitcher and catcher both."

Willie's standings went down that year, though not very far. His batting average was .296, with 36 home runs and 84 runs-batted-in. He led the league with 40 stolen bases. No National League player had ever before stolen more than 30 bases and also hit more than 30 homers in the same season.

"Willie and Jackie Robinson can both make a game come alive just by getting on base," one sportswriter said.

But the Giants ended up in sixth place. Their chances for 1957 looked grim too. Several players were past their peak. The rookies weren't seasoned enough. A lot of people said, "I told you so!" when the Giants landed in sixth place again.

But, again, nobody blamed Willie Mays.

"He looked as if he were trying to win the pennant all by himself," somebody said.

In one game Willie had been on first when the next batter tapped out a grounder. The batter was out at first. But Willie had taken off with the swing of the bat, and he made it all the way to third. There he danced around until he upset the pitcher. Then he stole home.

In the All-Star game he had played with a limp because of a leg injury. But he batted .500 that day, getting a single and a triple and driving in two of his team's five runs.

He stole 38 bases that season, to lead both leagues. He hit 35 home runs. His 20 triples set a record for three-base hits in one season. He won the slugging championship for the third time in four years.

And his .333 batting average put him right behind the year's top man, Stan Musial.

The downhill course of the Giants was proved by emptying stands. The Giants had drawn a million and a half fans in 1954. By 1957 less than half that number were turning up.

Horace Stoneham decided his team needed a new home.

This sequence shows Willie in top form as he steals third base and romps home.

"We're moving to San Francisco," the Giants' owner said. "We'll draw bigger crowds there."

Willie loved New York and didn't want to leave it. New Yorkers didn't want to lose him.

When he came to the plate in the ninth inning of the season's last New York game, the fans rose to cheer him. They knew they would probably never again see Willie Mays in a New York Giants uniform. They wanted him to know how much they loved him.

They went on cheering even when the pitcher started to throw. Willie understood what they were telling him. He stepped out of the box and touched his cap in a farewell salute.

Then he stepped back into the box and grounded out. But the fans' cheers still followed him as he jogged back to the dugout.

72

7. A Rough Time

The first time Willie Mays walked out on the field as a San Francisco Giant, the fans booed him. They booed him often after that.

"Why?" Willie asked the reporters.

"They think you're trying to take the place of their hometown hero, DiMaggio," one said.

"But he retired six years ago!" Willie said. "Besides, he was my hero too. I wouldn't try to take his place."

"They think we invented your great reputation," a New York writer said. "Don't worry. You'll prove yourself to them."

"But they cheer Cepeda," Willie said. "And he hasn't had time to prove himself yet."

Orlando Cepeda was the Giants' rookie first baseman.

"They feel he belongs to them, because he's starting out here," a third writer said. "They say 'Cepeda's not one of those imported New York stars.'"

Willie met unfriendliness away from the field too. When he and his wife were buying a house, the owner suddenly called off the sale.

"Blacks aren't welcome in that neighborhood," someone told Willie.

The mayor of San Francisco was so ashamed of his city that he invited the Mays family to stay in his own home. The owner of the house Willie wanted decided to sell to him after all.

But poison-pen letters came in the mail. One night a bottle crashed through a window. Finally Willie moved his family back to New York, for safety. After that he lived alone during the baseball season.

He had always been a fierce competitor on the diamond. But he had never been thrown out of a game for fighting other players or for arguing with umpires.

"That's a waste of energy," he always said. "I like to save mine for playing ball."

Now he thought it would be a waste of energy to fight the people of San Francisco. Many blacks believed he was wrong to feel that way. So Willie explained his ideas about overcoming discrimination. He said, "The old generation can't ever change. You have to wait for the young generation. I think sports has helped a lot. I think sports will help a lot more."

And he continued trying to keep his mind on his job as a ballplayer. He even learned to outguess the famous San

Mays socks one out to center field in San Francisco.

Francisco wind that could suddenly blow foul balls fair and fair balls foul.

The Giants ended in third place in 1958, but Willie's .347 batting average was his highest ever. He had hit 29 homers and batted in 96 runs. His 208 hits and 31 stolen bases led the league.

In the next year the Giants just missed the pennant. Willie had suffered a lot of injuries, but for the fourth straight year he led the league with 27 stolen bases. He hit 34 homers, drove in 104 runs, and batted .313.

Even on the day he broke his finger, he got a double and two singles. In the All-Star contest he slammed the three-bagger that won the game.

"The only man who could have caught it, hit it," a reporter wrote about that drive.

By 1960 the fans were still giving their loudest cheers to Cepeda. "But Willie's the team's solid core," they finally admitted. "Maybe he'll lead us to a pennant this year."

The Giants did start out like winners. But they fell apart at the end of the season and ended in fifth place. Willie hit .319 and was the only Giant to hit over .300 that year.

Stoneham named Alvin Dark as the Giant manager for 1961. Dark had played shortstop on the 1951 pennant-winning team with rookie Willie Mays.

"Knowing you will be playing for me,"

Dark wrote to Willie, "is the greatest privilege and thrill any manager could hope to have." He also built Willie up with the reporters at every opportunity.

"He gives me a real lift," Willie said.

Willie needed that lift. He and his wife were not getting along very well, and they were having money problems. Both were extravagant, and the house in New York had cost a lot. For some time now Willie had been borrowing money from his employers to help cover his expenses.

The Giants started out strong under Dark and moved up into first place. Willie came out of a brief spring slump in a game against Milwaukee on April 30. In that one game he hit four home runs! Only eight other men had ever done that in the history of baseball.

In July the Giants went back to New York to play an exhibition game against the Yankees. Fifty thousand fans roared

The Say-Hey Kid gets a warm welcome from
the bleacher fans at a New York game. New
Yorkers still considered Willie their own.

their welcome to Willie when his name was announced in the lineup. They hadn't forgotten him.

But in spite of their good start, and Willie's .308 average and 40 homers, the Giants wound up in third place. They were determined not to let the flag get away from them the next year.

A first-time-up homer against Warren Spahn started the 1962 season for Willie. The Giants beat the Braves 6–0 that day.

Then things got rough. For Willie they got very rough. He and his wife had agreed on a divorce. It meant Willie would see less of their little adopted son Michael. It also meant more big expenses.

To add to Willie's troubles, the Giants asked him to repay the money he owed them. Even though Willie earned $90,000 that year, it was not enough to cover everything.

Finally a banker worked out a program that let Willie meet his obligations and pay his debts. Willie promised himself never to get into financial trouble again.

He had to rest four days in a hospital that season. The Giants lost four games while he was out. But their Dodger rivals lost some games too. It was a neck-and-neck race down to the very end.

On the season's last day Willie's eighth-inning homer gave the Giants a win over Houston. That tied them with the Dodgers for the pennant.

Once more, as in 1951, the two teams faced a three-game play-off. The stands were jammed for the first game. People were glued to their television screens.

Willie hit two homers. The Giants won 8–0.

The Dodgers won the second game. And the Dodgers were ahead as the third game went into the ninth. The score was 4–2 with full bases when Willie came up to bat. The ball sped from the mound. Willie swung. The ball sizzled straight back to the pitcher, bounced off his leg, and went into center field for a single and a score. Two more runs that inning made it Giants 6, Dodgers 4.

Then the Giants held the Dodgers scoreless during their half. Willie caught a line drive for the last out. The Giants were the National League champions.

Thirty thousand San Franciscans were at the airport when their team came home. This time their loudest cheers were for Willie Mays.

Even when the New York Yankees took the World Series, the city's enthusiasm wasn't dampened.

That fall Willie bought a new house in San Francisco. His son Michael could visit him there, and his father and one of his half brothers could live with him. He was finally at home among the fans who had booed him for so long.

8. "Willie's Back!"

Willie gave his fans plenty to cheer about in 1963. He batted .314. His 38 home runs brought his lifetime total to 406.

The next year he became the Giants' captain—the first black captain in the major leagues. This added job meant more responsibilities. And injuries were making him feel his age. His averages dropped.

"You planning to retire soon?" people asked.

"Not as long as I can help the team," Willie always answered.

Willie is greeted at the plate (above) after hitting the 521st home run of his career. The great slugger hit his 607th in the photograph at the left.

Herman Franks, the new Giant manager, didn't want to lose him. Together they worked out plans to give Willie more rest. And in 1965, 34-year-old Willie played as if he were 24 again.

On July 8 he hit homer 23, the 476th of his career. That beat the lifetime record of Stan Musial. In August alone he hit 17 home runs! On September 13 he slammed out number 500. When he hit his season's 52nd, on the last day of play, he set a new record for himself and for the Giants. And to top off that great year, he won his second Most Valuable Player award.

In May of 1966 he drove out number 512 to become his league's all-time home-run champion. In June he passed Ted Williams's record. His number 535 beat the record of Jimmy Foxx. Now only the great Babe Ruth had hit more home runs than Willie Mays.

From then on the homers came more

slowly. There were days when injuries and fatigue kept Willie off the field. There were days when he wished he weren't playing. His hard brand of baseball took a lot out of him. But he wouldn't give up.

On the opening day of the 1969 season, Willie stole second base—and the game stopped dead. It was his 300th steal! While the fans cheered, the sack was removed and given to Willie as a memento of the occasion.

Late that season the Giants were facing the San Diego Padres. Willie, tired and in pain, was on the bench. But when the game was tied in the seventh, he went in to pinch hit.

The ball came at him. He swung with all the old Mays power. The ball ended up in the stands. The scoreboard flashed a big 600!

Teammates, fans, and sportswriters crowded around him as he left the field.

Everyone wanted to celebrate his history-making homer.

"But the big thing isn't that it was number 600," Willie said. "The big thing is that it won the game."

In May 1971 the whole world of baseball congratulated Willie Mays on his 40th birthday. A big dinner in his honor earned money for his favorite charity, a boys' club.

He played 136 games that season. His average was a respectable .271. His 18 homers and 61 runs-batted-in helped push the Giants to top place in their division.

Willie knew that few ballplayers play well after the age of 40. He knew the $150,000-a-year contract he now had with the Giants would end in 1972. And he knew Stoneham was not likely to offer him another like it, because gate receipts were falling.

In the meantime the New York Mets

Willie takes a look at Shea Stadium, his new home in baseball, from the press box.

had been trying to buy Willie's contract. Stoneham decided the time had come when the Mets could do more for Willie than he could. He and the Mets owner reached an agreement. It said Willie would go on receiving his big salary from the Mets for as long as he remained an active player. Then, if he wished, he could remain with the Mets in a non-playing job for ten more years at $75,000 a year.

88

When Willie heard about the plan, he was glad and sorry at the same time. He was sorry to leave the Giants. "But it will be good to get back to New York," he said.

And he would not be facing the future alone. He had just married pretty Mae Allen, a social worker.

"Willie's back!" The words that had greeted him on his return from the army now greeted him again, all over New York.

Signs in shop and house windows, newspaper headlines and ads, all said, "Welcome home, Willie!" People wore buttons that read "Say-Hey!"

The stands went crazy the first time Willie trotted onto Shea Stadium field in his Mets uniform. His old number 24 was on his back.

"We want Willie!" people shouted.

Yogi Berra, the Mets manager, said, "I'll use him when the right spot comes up."

Berra waited two days until Sunday, May 14, 1972. The Mets were playing Willie's old team, the Giants.

Willie took a walk his first time at bat. The screams of the fans followed him as he trotted toward first.

In the fifth inning the game was tied 4–4. Willie came up to bat for the third time. The count went to three and two. Then he smacked the ball for a homer that won the game!

"It's a good thing Shea Stadium is made of steel and concrete," one sportswriter said, "or the fans would have ripped the place apart with their enthusiasm."

In his first 27 trips to the plate, Willie got on base 14 times. By early June he had won three games for the Mets, two with homers, one with a fourteenth-inning single.

On July 21 he was back in the Giants' Candlestick Park, in San Francisco. Once

Mays was off to a sensational start with a game-winning home run in his first appearance as a Met. Below, Willie slides home safely in a game with the Expos several days later.

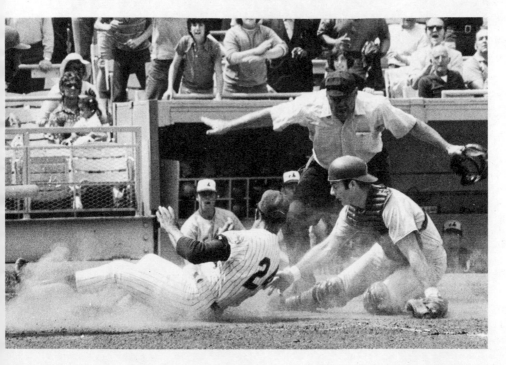

more the Mets were playing the Giants. No one cheered him more loudly than the once-unfriendly Giant fans. And again Willie slammed out a homer to bring the Mets another of their scarce victories that year.

The very next day he appeared in his 23rd All-Star game as the senior man on the field.

Injuries kept the Mets low in the ratings that year. Late in the season Willie had his own share. Even the winter's rest didn't help. He went on the disabled list the next spring for the first time in his career.

"Is he finished?" people wondered.

Willie himself was finally talking of retiring. But he put off a decision. Again injuries were giving the Mets a rough year. He knew he was needed. He was back on the field as soon as he could play.

His fans poured out to cheer him in every city on the Mets' schedule.

"This may be our last chance to see Willie play," they said.

At the end of August, with the Mets in last place, several of their best players finally recovered. Then the team took off. In less than three weeks it was close to the top.

But Willie had cracked three ribs in a fall.

"And at 42 you can't play the way you could at 20, anyway," he said.

He had played well enough that year to raise his home-run total to 660. Only Babe Ruth and Henry Aaron have hit more.

But at Shea Stadium, on September 21, 1973, Willie Mays announced that he would retire at the end of the season. Reporters and photographers crowded around him. Once more his words and his picture flooded the news.

"I thought I'd be crying right now," Willie admitted, "but so many people love

**The great baseball star's last time at bat in
a major-league game—October 16, 1973**

me that I don't hurt too bad. Maybe I'll cry tomorrow."

After a frantic five-game play-off with the Cincinnati Reds, the Mets took their first pennant since 1969. On October 13 they met the Oakland A's in the World Series.

A standing ovation honored Willie Mays as he took center field for his fourth World Series. He was playing in Oakland Stadium, which he had never seen before.

His first time at bat, he sent a sharp single through the hole past third base. He had made the first hit of the Series!

"He had to get a hit," Mets pitcher, Ray Sadecki, said. "This game was invented for Willie Mays!"

Willie's second and last Series hit helped the Mets to one of their three victories. The Series went to seven games before they lost. Willie didn't play after the third game, but he was always on hand. And at every game there were homemade banners in the stands reading, "We want Willie!"

When the Series ended, Willie was ready to go home and relax. He had earned a rest. He would be back the next year as a coach. His teammates would still have the help of his skills and experience. But the fans would no longer see him on the field. They would miss him.

"I was an infant when Willie became a star," Cleon Jones, a Met fielder, said. "And he was already Number One. That is, there was nobody else. Nobody."

The sportswriters would miss him too.

"Never another like him," sportswriter Red Smith wrote. "Never in this world."